D1120122

CALGARY PUBLIC LIBRARY
DECEMBER 2012

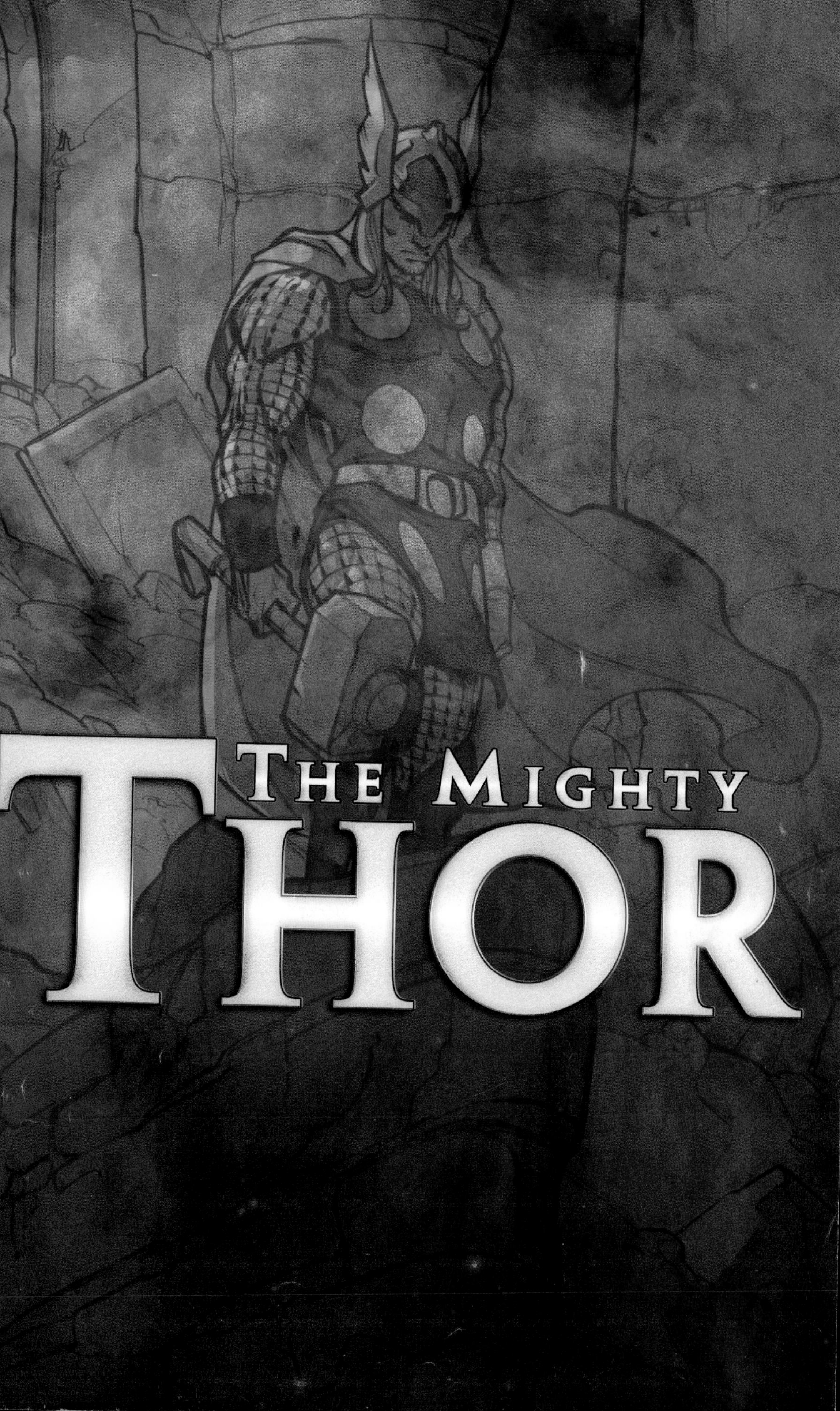

THE MIGHTY THOR

COLLECTION EDITOR: JENNIFER GRÜNWALD · ASSISTANT EDITORS: ALEX STARBUCK & NELSON RIBEIRO
EDITOR, SPECIAL PROJECTS: MARK D. BEAZLEY · SENIOR EDITOR, SPECIAL PROJECTS: JEFF YOUNGQUIST
SENIOR VICE PRESIDENT OF SALES: DAVID GABRIEL
SVP OF BRAND PLANNING & COMMUNICATIONS: MICHAEL PASCIULLO

EDITOR IN CHIEF: AXEL ALONSO · CHIEF CREATIVE OFFICER: JOE QUESADA
PUBLISHER: DAN BUCKLEY · EXECUTIVE PRODUCER: ALAN FINE

THE MIGHTY THOR BY MATT FRACTION VOL. 3. Contains material originally published in magazine form as THE MIGHTY THOR #12.1 and #13-17. First printing 2012. Hardcover ISBN# 978-0-7851-6166-0. Softcover ISBN# 978-0-7851-6167-7. Published by MARVEL WORLDWIDE, INC., a subsidiary of MARVEL ENTERTAINMENT, LLC. OFFICE OF PUBLICATION: 135 West 50th Street, New York, NY 10020. Copyright © 2012 Marvel Charact All rights reserved. Hardcover: $24.99 per copy in the U.S. and $27.99 in Canada (GST #R127032852). Softcover: $19.99 per copy in the U.S. and $21.99 in Canada (GST #R127032852). Canadian Agreement #406 All characters featured in this issue and the distinctive names and likenesses thereof, and all related indicia are trademarks of Marvel Characters, Inc. No similarity between any of the names, characters, persons institutions in this magazine with those of any living or dead person or institution is intended, and any such similarity which may exist is purely coincidental. **Printed in the U.S.A.** ALAN FINE, EVP - Office of the President Worldwide, Inc. and EVP & CMO Marvel Characters B.V.; DAN BUCKLEY, Publisher & President - Print, Animation & Digital Divisions; JOE QUESADA, Chief Creative Officer; TOM BREVOORT, SVP of Publishing; DAVID BOGA of Operations & Procurement, Publishing; RUWAN JAYATILLEKE, SVP & Associate Publisher, Publishing; C.B. CEBULSKI, SVP of Creator & Content Development; DAVID GABRIEL, SVP of Publishing Sales & Circulation; M PASCIULLO, SVP of Brand Planning & Communications; JIM O'KEEFE, VP of Operations & Logistics; DAN CARR, Executive Director of Publishing Technology; SUSAN CRESPI, Editorial Operations Manager; ALEX M Publishing Operations Manager; STAN LEE, Chairman Emeritus. For information regarding advertising in Marvel Comics or on Marvel.com, please contact Niza Disla, Director of Marvel Partnerships, at ndisla@mar For Marvel subscription inquiries, please call 800-217-9158. **Manufactured between 7/30/2012 and 9/10/2012 (hardcover), and 7/30/2012 and 3/11/2013 (softcover), by R.R. DONNELLEY, INC., SALEM,**

10 9 8 7 6 5 4 3 2 1

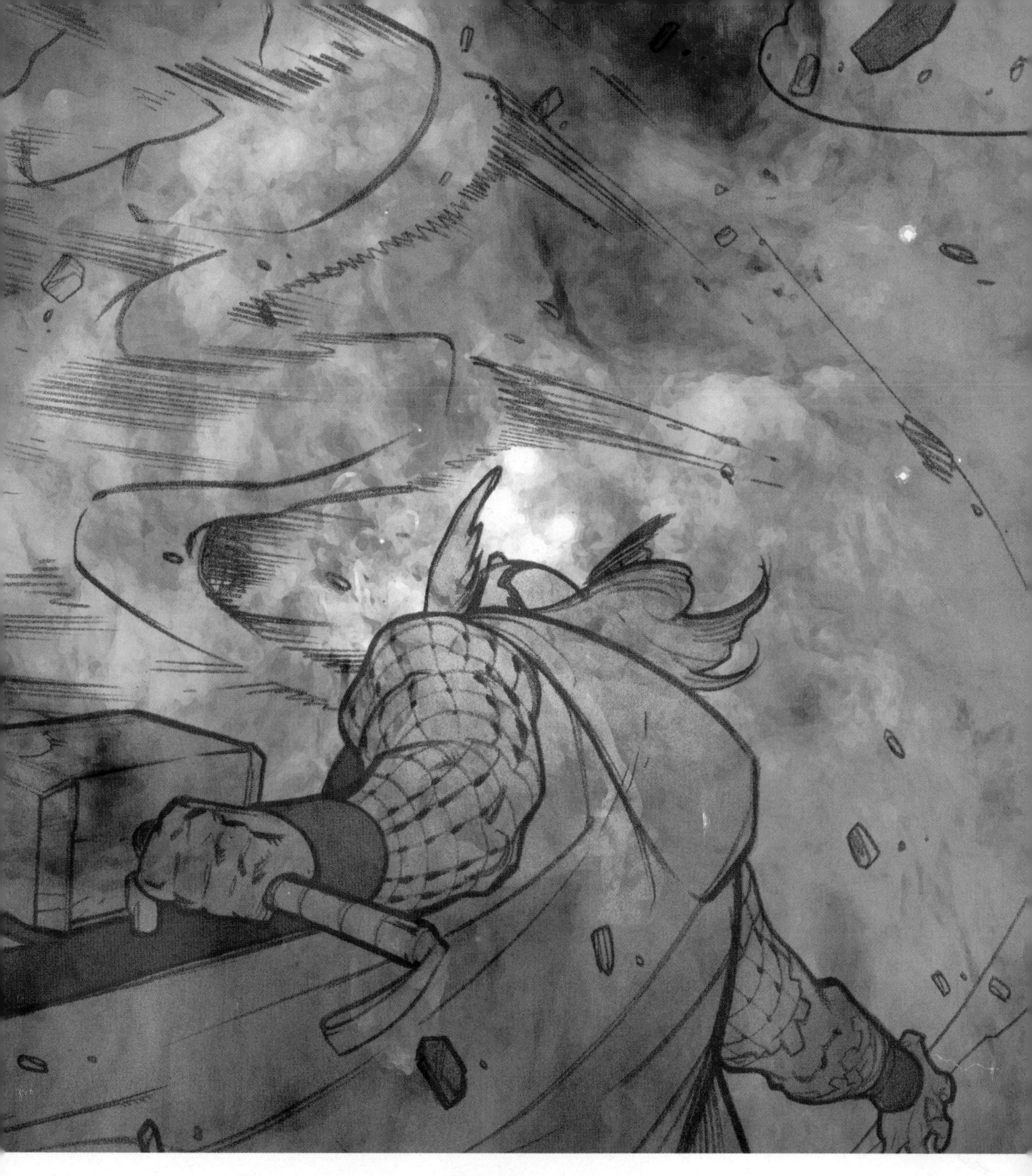

WRITER
MATT FRACTION

ARTISTS
BARRY KITSON WITH **JAY LEISTEN** (#12.1)
& **PEPE LARRAZ** (#13-17)

COLOR ARTISTS
FRANK D'ARMATA (#12.1-16) & **WIL QUINTANA** (#17)

LETTERER
VC'S JOE SABINO

COVER ART
OLIVIER COIPEL WITH **LAURA MARTIN** (#12.1)
AND **WALTER SIMONSON** WITH **PAUL MOUNTS** & **LAURA MARTIN** (#13-17)

ASSISTANT EDITOR
JOHN DENNING

EDITOR
LAUREN SANKOVITCH

12.1

He is the son of Asgard, a golden city floating high above the Earth's surface, the capital of a new republic of Nine Worlds led by the All-Mother.
He is the God of Thunder. He is an Avenger. He is—

The Mighty Thor

THOR

SIF

VOLSTAGG

LOKI

SIF, YOU SEE, THE THING TO CONSIDER REGARDING THOR...
...HE'S AN ELDER BROTHER. A PROTECTOR. ALWAYS HAS BEEN; ALWAYS WILL--
--BE!
VOLSTAGG THE VOLUMINOUS. OF ALL THE PEOPLE TO SAY ALL THE THINGS--
--STEADY, GIRL--
--YOU FEEL COMPELLED TO TELL ME THAT?
"AS RARELY AS I HAVE NEEDED IT, AND AS OFTEN AS IT HAS INFURIATED ME...
"I HAVE KNOW IT OF THOR FOR AGES."

"...EVEN BEFORE HE WAS GRANTED THAT DAMNED HAMMER, EVEN BEFORE HIS FALL AND RISE.
"AS A MAN BARELY OUT OF BOYHOOD IT WAS CLEAR WHO HE WAS.
"AND WHAT HE WOULD BECOME...
AGNAR, THE HALF-KING OF EAGLES, SENT THE AERIE LEGION TO ATTACK THE ALL-GODDESS IDUNN AS SHE HARVESTED HER GOLDEN APPLES.
"I WAS SUPPOSED TO BE PROTECTING HER. I WAS A GIRL, BARELY A WOMAN, LET ALONE A WARRIOR AND IDUNN WAS CONSIDERED UNTOUCHABLE.
"AGNAR'S AUDACIOUSNESS ONLY BENEFITED FROM MY YOUTH.
"I FAILED.
"WHEN THOR ARRIVED I THOUGHT HE WAS SIMPLY ATTACKING AGNAR LIKE A PURE WILD ANIMAL.
"ALL VIOLENCE AND CHAOS. NO STRATEGY.

"I WAS WRONG."
LOKI, NOW--!
--TRYING--
"WHETHER OR NOT IT WAS HIS PLAN OR HIS BROTHER LOKI'S--
"--AND, VOLSTAGG, LET US BE HONEST, AT THAT POINT IN HIS LIFE IT COULD HAVE BEEN EITHER--
"--IT WORKED.

"FOR ALL HIS CUNNING THUS DID AGNAR THE HALF-BREED AIR COLOSSUS FALL.
"THUS DID HE FACE THOR'S WRATH FOR DARING TO MEDDLE WITH THE GOLDEN APPLES OF ASGARD...
"THUS DID HE FACE LOKI'S TREACHERY.

"DID THOR PROTECT ASGARD? WAS HE HER TRUE GUARDIAN THAT DAY?
"OF THAT I HAVE NO DOUBT.

"BUT THE TREACHERY OF THE THING--THE TRICKERY OF THE DEED--
"IT FELT OUT OF PLACE FOR THOR-THE-PROTECTOR...

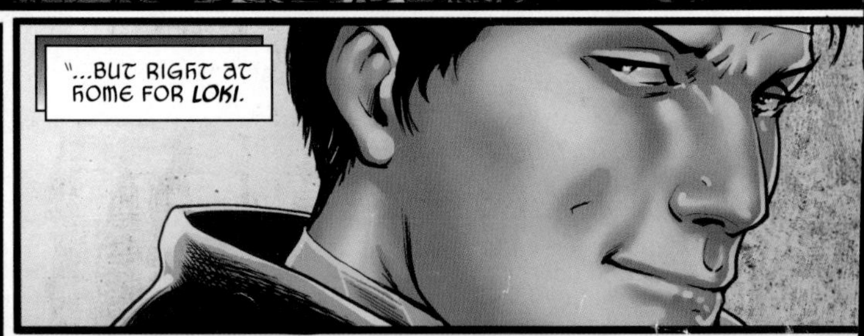
"...BUT RIGHT AT HOME FOR LOKI.

"I'VE NO DOUBT THOR COULD HAVE STORMED AGNAR WITH NOTHING MORE THAN RAGE AND TWO SWORDS TO THE SAME RESULT...
"AND YET HIS RESCUE REQUIRED THAT FEINT.
"STILL...
"HE REMAINED-- AND REMAINS-- SO INEFFABLY..."
...THOR.

BAH. AS THOUGH I NEED REMINDING THAT THOR IS A GOOD MAN.

HE LEARNED IT FROM ME!
NOW EVERYTHING IS PERFECT. HE AND I SHARE A BOND, WOMAN. A BOND.

OH YOU DO, DO YOU?

WOMAN!
I KNOW THAT TONE. I RECOGNIZE THE SUBTLE DERISION, THE IMPLIED SARCASM.
AND I HAVE HEARD IT ALL BEFORE. BUT KNOW THIS...

"THOR AND I SHARE A BOND NO ONE WILL EVER UNDERSTAND...
"AND IT HAUNTS ME NOW AS IT DID THEN...
"...WHEN I WAS KNOWN AS VOLSTAGG THE STAGGERINGLY PERFECT."

WE WERE IN HEL. AT THE THRESHOLD BETWEEN IT AND ASGARD...
WELL, BOYS?
THE FIVE OF US TO STAND TOGETHER, EH?
I SHALL STAND BEHIND IF NONE OBJECTS...
AGAINST ALL THE GATHERED HORDES OF HEL! WITH NO WAY TO ALERT OUR BROTHERS! NO AID COMING, NO RELIEF!
WE'LL BE HOME IN TIME FOR THE EVENING'S FEAST.
"I WAS SO YOUNG. WE ALL WERE. BUT WITH MY YOUTH AND...RESPLENDENT PHYSICAL FORM, SIF, CAME CONFIDENCE.
"UNEARNED CONFIDENCE. IMPOSSIBLE, UNSHAKABLE... AND STUPID.

"FORTY DAYS AND FORTY NIGHTS WE STOOD ALONE AGAINST THE GATHERED LEGIONS OF THE DAMNED AND DOOMED.

"WITHOUT FOOD. WITHOUT DRINK. WITHOUT SLEEP.

"IMAGINE THAT, SIF. IN A LAND WITH NO DAY AND NO NIGHT BUT JUST HEAT AND MISERY...

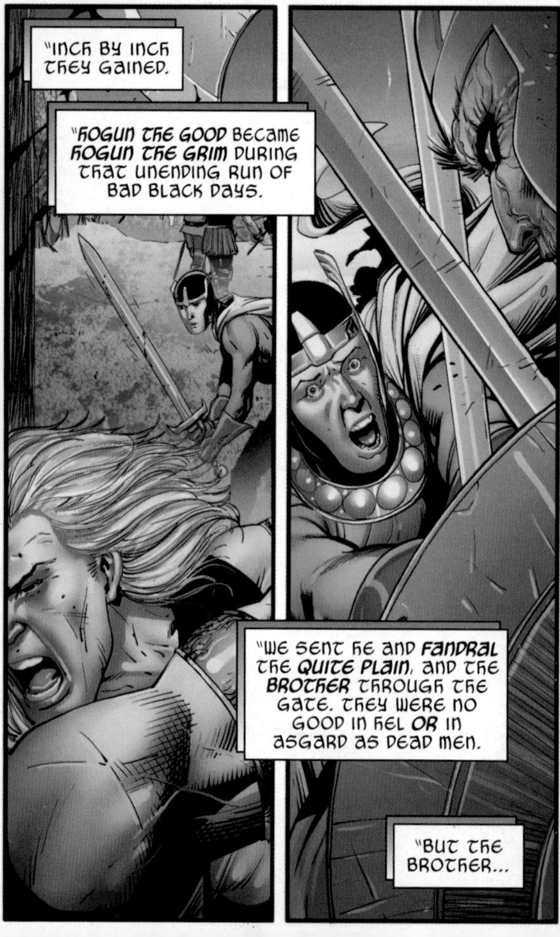
"INCH BY INCH THEY GAINED.
"HOGUN THE GOOD BECAME HOGUN THE GRIM DURING THAT UNENDING RUN OF BAD BLACK DAYS.
"WE SENT HE AND FANDRAL THE QUITE PLAIN, AND THE BROTHER THROUGH THE GATE. THEY WERE NO GOOD IN HEL OR IN ASGARD AS DEAD MEN.
"BUT THE BROTHER...

"...REFUSED.
"AND SO STILL WE FOUGHT. TOOTH AND NAIL.
"THEN--

"TRAGEDY!"

"THIS WAS BEFORE THE BOY HAD THE HAMMER, MIND.
"THIS WAS BEFORE SO MANY THINGS.

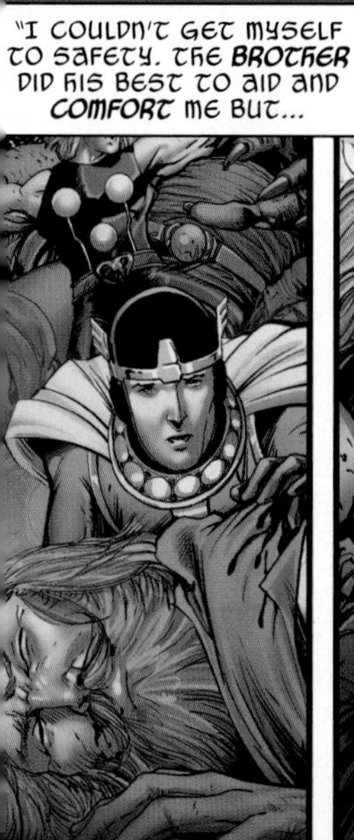
"I COULDN'T GET MYSELF TO SAFETY. THE BROTHER DID HIS BEST TO AID AND COMFORT ME BUT...

"...BUT I COULD ONLY SLUMP THERE AND BLEED AND STARVE AND STARE.

"HE FOUGHT ALONE FOR FORTY MORE DAYS, SIF.
"AND WHEN IT WAS DONE...

"THE STUDENT HAD BECOME THE TEACHER.

"THE BOY PICKED ME UP AND CARRIED ME TO SAFETY.
"EIGHTY DAYS WITHOUT FOOD. I STARTED EATING AS SOON AS I COULD SIT UPRIGHT AGAIN AND HAVEN'T STOPPED SINCE."
I HAD SEEN THE VERY BEST OF US IN HIM, SIF.

AND THAT WAS BEFORE HE HAD MJOLNIR?
I BELIEVE THAT WAS WHAT EARNED HIM THE HAMMER, IN THE EYE OF ODIN...

...AND HIS VICTORIES BECAME EVEN BIGGER. EVEN MORE GLORIOUS AFTER THAT...
AYE, THEY DID AT THAT, AS DID HIS BLOODLUST--

--SPEAKING OF THE HAMMER, RECALL YOU THE DOOMED THRYMR OF JOTUNKIND?

THE GREAT THIEF OF JOTNAR AND THE GREAT OTHER POSSESSOR OF MJOLNIR?

"IT STARTED WITH A SOUND SO LOUD I BELIEVED THE SKY ITSELF HAD CRACKED IN TWO.
"IT WAS THOR...

"...and he
s angry..."
Thor...
Calm down.
Calm
down?
CALM
DOWN?!
The
hammer is
lost, Balder.
The hammer
is gone.
Mjolnir.
The Crusher.
Forged by the
sons of Ivaldi
and blessed by
Odin himself--
-gone!
anished!
How? By
whom? And
where? Do you
nderstand what
a weapon of its
might loose in
the nine realms
may mean?
Organize
search parties.
I shall tear the
nine worlds
apart to--
Ahem.
I...
may...
...have
heard rumor
and whisper
regarding the
hammer's new
owner.

Thrymr.
And
he doesn't
really
want the
hammer...

"HE WANTS A BRIDE...!"
"LOKI HAD, NO DOUBT THROUGH ONE DAMN TRICK OR ANOTHER, SEEN TO IT THAT THE HAMMER MJOLNIR HAD FALLEN INTO THE VILE HANDS OF THRYMR, KING OF FROST...
"...AND HE HAD RANSOM IN MIND. THE HAMMER FOR THE HAND OF FREYJA, THOR'S OWN MOTHER. SO LOKI CAME UP WITH A SCHEME..."
I FEEL MY VERY BLOOD BOIL.
GOOD! EXCELLENT! WE CAN USE THAT, THOR. WE CAN--
SHUT UP.
YOU ARE RIGHT, THOR, PERHAPS SILENCE IS BEST. 'TIS TIME FOR MEDITATIVE FOCUS. TO CHANNEL YOUR RAGE INTO A PLAN OF ACTION. BESIDES...

WE'RE REACHED THE HALL OF THRYMR AND...
...AND IT DOES RATHER LOOK LIKE THEY'RE EXPECTING A WEDDING.
"THUS DID THE SONS OF ODIN INFILTRATE THAT AWFUL PLACE. AND THUS DID THOR, HIS VEIL KEPT DOWN, AND LOKI, HIS SILVER-SPEAKING DEMON'S TONGUE WAGGING, INVADE.
"AN ARMY OF TWO, ONE OF WHOM HAD COME TO MARRY THE KING OF ALL-FROST."

TELL ME, HANDMAIDEN:
DOES SHE LOOK ODD TO YOU? HER APPETITE SEEMS... VORACIOUS...
NO, NO, MY LORD, SURELY 'TIS BUT WEDDING NIGHT NERVES!

"MILORD WILL FORGIVE MY IMPROPRIETY BUT I WOULD WAGER FREYJA WISHES TO BE STRONG AND READY FOR YOU..."
MMPPH.
MORE.

READY YOURSELF, WOMAN. CONSUMMATION IS AT HAND.
"THUS IN THE BRIDEGROOM'S CHAMBERS WERE THOR AND HIS HAMMER REUNITED...
FREYJA? I HEARD BREAKING GLASS.
WHY DO YOU HOLD THE HAMMER OF YOUR SON?
FREYJA?
BRIDE?
OR KILLED HIM, F COURSE.
EN HE KILLED ALL OF THE ST GIANTS IN THRYMR'S LL. THE GUESTS, THE NITARIES, ALL OF THEM.
"HE'D KILLED HALF THE REALM BEFORE WE CALMED HIM DOWN."

HA HA HA HA HA HA HA!

PERHAPS ONE HAD TO BE PRESENT TO FIND THE HUMOR.
NOT THAT I WAS PRESENT.
IN SPIRIT, MIND, BUT--
VOLSTAGG.

THOR WASN'T SO EMBARRASSED...
...WELL. OF COURSE HE WAS, BUT--
AH.

HIS IRE WAS CONNECTED TO HIS FEALTY TO BLOOD.
HAD THAT DUMB FROST GIANT DEMANDED THE HAND OF ANYONE ELSE IN ASGARD OTHER THAN THOR'S MOTHER...

WRONG THE FAMILY OF THE ODINBORN AND THERE WILL BE BLOOD, BY GOD.

"IN FACT...
"...IT WAS VIOLENCE PERPETRATED UPON LOKI THAT IGNITED THOR'S GREATEST FURY..."
HUUHH--
WHO GOES THERE?

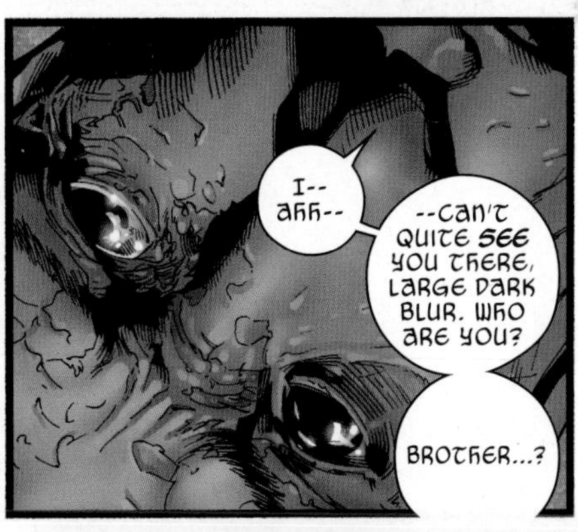

I-- AHH--
--CAN'T QUITE SEE YOU THERE, LARGE DARK BLUR. WHO ARE YOU?
BROTHER...?

WHO...
...DID THIS...
...TO YOU?!

BROTHER, LOOK OUT-

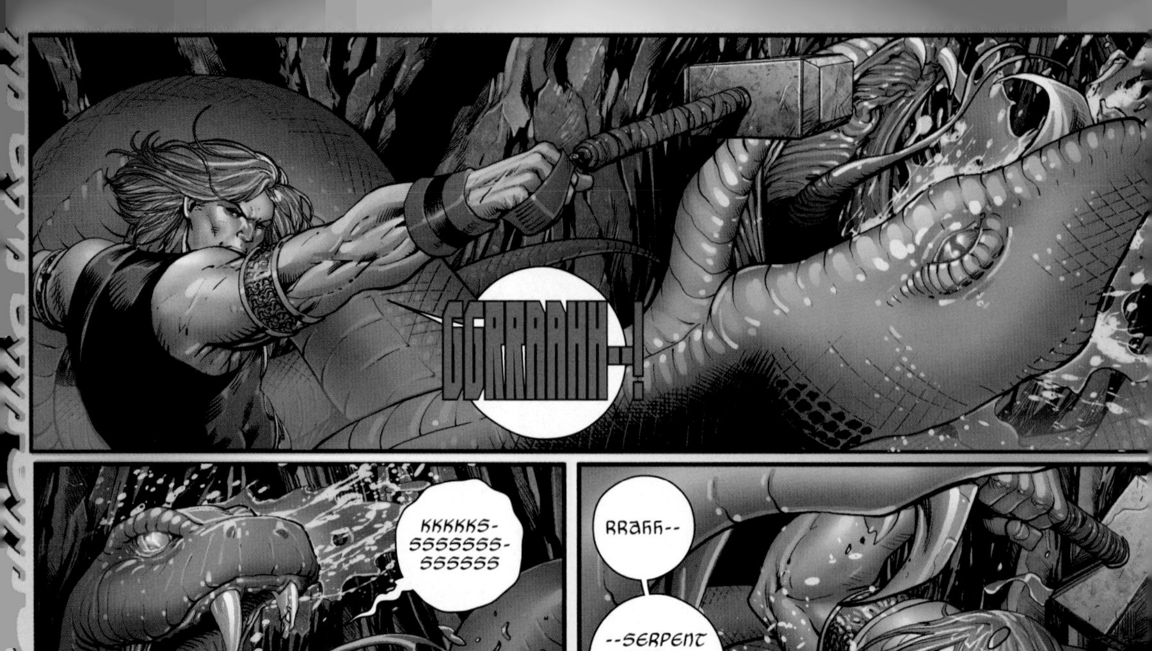
GGRRAAHH--!

KKKKKS-
SSSSSSS-
SSSSSS
SHUT YOUR MOUTH FOR YOU--

RRAHH--
--SERPENT YOU-- AAAAH--
--YOU BORE ME AS--
--AS IT HAS BEEN PROPHESIZED DIE FIGHTING A SERPENT...

...IT WILL NOT BE TODAY.

"TO FIND LOKI IN SUCH A DEBASED STATE ENRAGED THOR, WHO NEVER ALLOWED HIMSELF TO WONDER IF THERE WAS ANY SORT OF CRIME THAT COULD FIT SUCH PUNISHMENT.
"ALL HE KNEW WAS THAT HIS BLOOD--IMAGINED BLOOD, AT THAT--WAS WRONGED."

YOUR PAIN IS AT AN END NOW, BROTHER, AND SO I ASK YOU AGAIN:
WHO DID THIS TO YOU?

"ODIN HAD. AND YET LOKI..."

ER...
"IN THAT MOMENT, VOLSTAGG--
"--IN THAT WHITE HOT MOMENT, THE PRINCE OF LIES DID WHAT HE DOES BEST:

"HE LIED."
FROST GIANTS.
BIG COLD BASTARDS CUT OUT SIGYN'S TONGUE TOO. NOW SHE'LL NEVER SPEAK AGAIN...

I SHALL KILL THEM ALL AND--
THOR, NO! WAIT!
THOR, THERE IS A TRUCE! A TREATY!

THINK FOR ONE MOMENT--
--I AM, LOKI--
--THEN THINK HARDER, DAMMIT. THINK LIKE A TRICKSTER FOR A MOMENT.

THERE IS VALUE TO SECRETS. LET THIS BE OURS. I SHALL HIDE FOR THE TIME BEING AND YOU...

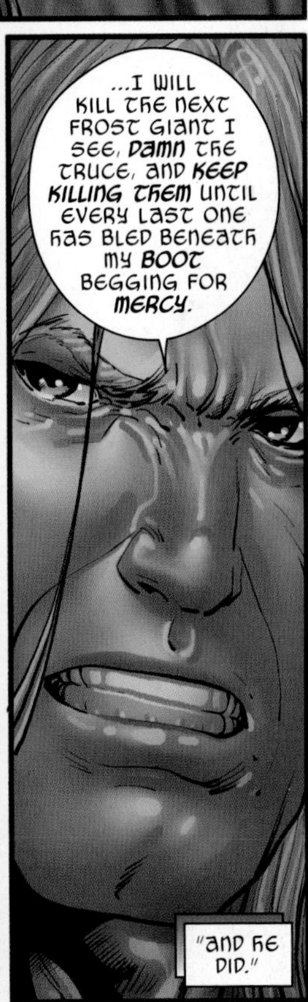
...I WILL KILL THE NEXT FROST GIANT I SEE, DAMN THE TRUCE, AND KEEP KILLING THEM UNTIL EVERY LAST ONE HAS BLED BENEATH MY BOOT BEGGING FOR MERCY.
"AND HE DID."

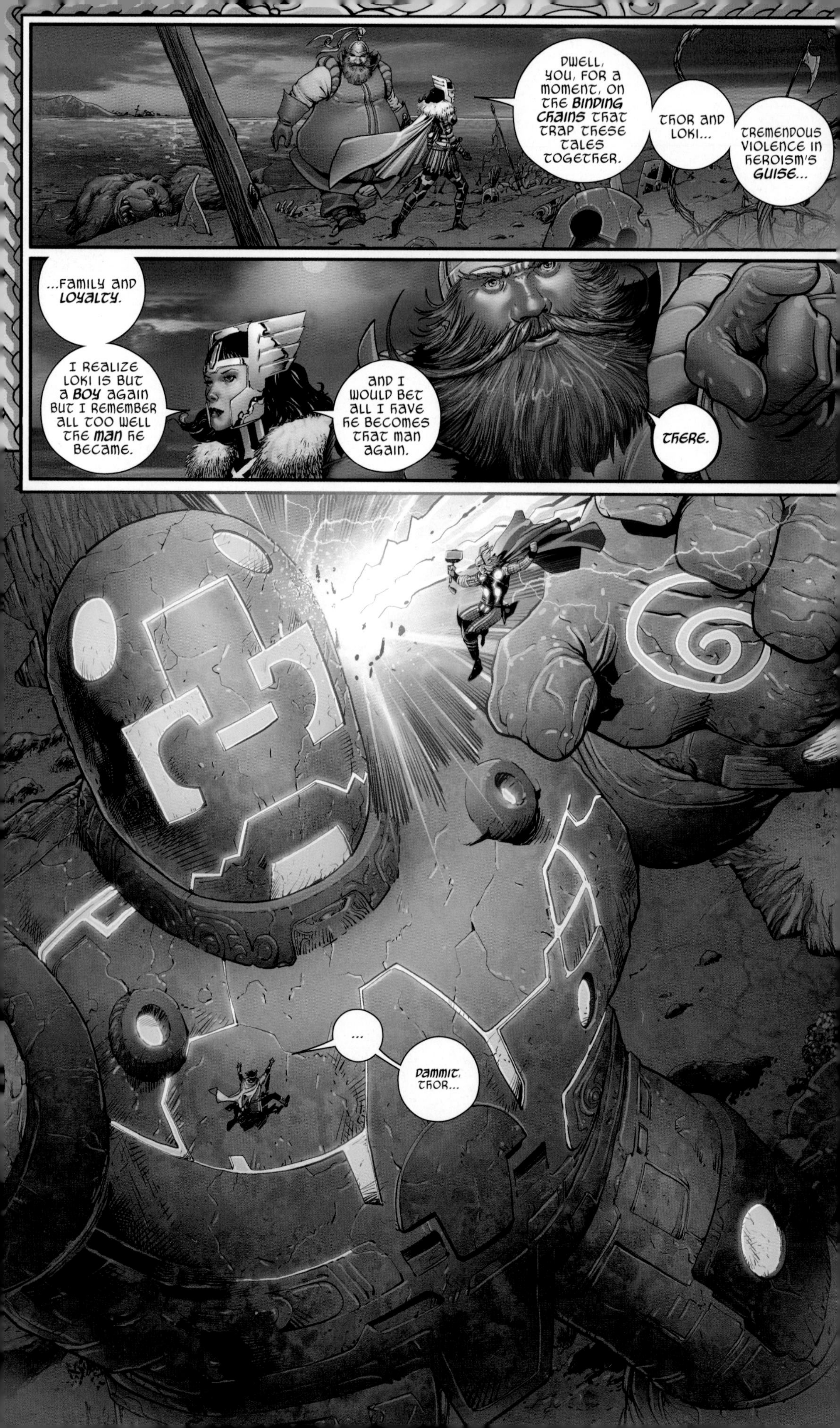
DWELL, YOU, FOR A MOMENT, ON THE BINDING CHAINS THAT TRAP THESE TALES TOGETHER.
THOR AND LOKI...
TREMENDOUS VIOLENCE IN HEROISM'S GUISE...
...FAMILY AND LOYALTY.
I REALIZE LOKI IS BUT A BOY AGAIN BUT I REMEMBER ALL TOO WELL THE MAN HE BECAME.
AND I WOULD BET ALL I HAVE HE BECOMES THAT MAN AGAIN.
THERE.
...
DAMMIT, THOR...

YOUR POINT--
JUST--
--BRAAAHHH!--
--DEAR WOMAN?

JUST THIS:
WHAT IF LOKI KNEW? WHAT IF LOKI WAS BEHIND THOR'S DOWNFALL ALL ALONG?
AFTER THAT THOR ATTACKED THE GIANT THAT LED TO ODIN CASTING HIM OUT. AND SO WHAT IF...
WHAT IF THE TRICKSTER WHO UNDID US ALL-- THE BOY WHO BECOMES THE MAN WHO UNLEASHES RAGNAROK ITSELF...

...HAS A BIG BROTHER THAT IS THE GREATEST WARRIOR IN THE NINE REALMS?
THANK YOU.
AYE.

YOU BELIEVE THOR'S HEROISM IS BEING WIELDED LIKE A WEAPON? THAT THOR IS BEING MANIPULATED BY THE CHILD?
NO, VOLSTAGG...

...I THINK WE ALL ARE.
HELLO DOWN THERE!

WE THOUGHT WE LOST YOU! HURRY UP!
YOU'RE ABOUT TO MISS THE BEST PART!
THOR'S ABOUT TO BASH THE FIEND'S HEAD IN!
STAR COLOSSUS. YOU AND YOUR HORDES--
--YOU HAVE RAMPAGED ACROSS OUR REALMS ENOUGH. WE HAVE CHASED YOU ENOUGH. THERE WILL BE NO MORE BLOOD SPILLED BY YOU AND YOURS TODAY.
RETURN TO WHERE YOU CAME OR FACE ULTIMATE SANCTION.
WAS HOPING FOR PRECISELY THAT RETORT, STAR DEMON...

LOOK OUT BELOW!
YESSSSS! AMAZING!
ANOTHER VICTORY-- ANOTHER EPIC VICTORY--
--ANOTHER EPIC, LEGENDARY, HEROIC VICTORY--
BY THE MIGHTY THOR!
EASY, BOY. SURELY SOMETHING SHALL STRAIN...
WORTH IT!
LONG LIVE THE MIGHTY THOR...!

13

OF ASGARD, A GOLDEN CITY FLOATING HIGH ABOVE THE EARTH'S SURFACE, THE
TAL OF A NEW REPUBLIC OF NINE WORLDS LED BY THE ALL-MOTHER.
HE IS THE GOD OF THUNDER. HE IS AN AVENGER. HE IS—

THE MIGHTY THOR

ED TO SAVE THE WORLD FROM FEAR ITSELF, AND ASGARD LAY
. BY BREAKING A SINISTER ENCHANTMENT, THOR RETURNED
E THE FLEDGLING REPUBLIC OF ASGARDIA FROM ITSELF, AND
AS RESTORED. THE WOULD-BE USURPERS OF THE RULING ALL-
HAVE BEEN UNDONE. THE CITY OF ASGARD HAS RETURNED TO
S, ITS FULL SPLENDOR RENEWED. THE NINE REALMS ARE CALM,
R THE GOD OF THUNDER, THAT CALM CAN ONLY MEAN THAT
SOMEWHERE, A STORM IS BREWING.

GO, AS A LESSON TO A YOUNG AND HEADSTRONG THOR, THE
THER JOINED THE THUNDER GOD TO THE MORTAL FORM OF
DONALD BLAKE TO TEACH THOR HUMILITY AND COMPASSION.

"THE GREATEST DAY OF MY ENTIRE LIFE?
"I FOUND A STICK IN A CAVE."
AND I'M A DOCTOR, SO...
...SO THAT WAS A PRETTY IMPORTANT STICK.

I ONLY HAVE TEN YEARS OF MEMORIES BEFORE THAT, WHICH TENDS TO MAKE DATES LIKE THIS ONE, THE WHOLE, THE WHOLE, THAT--
--THAT GETTING-TO-KNOW-YOU THING PRETTY SIMPLE.
I'M SORRY. YOU...WHAT?
I WAS TWENTY-ONE YEARS OLD WHEN I STARTED HAVING REAL MEMORIES. EXPERIENCES.
SEPTEMBER NINTH OF MY TWENTY-FIRST YEAR.
I REMEMBER BECAUSE...
"...UM.
"WELL, IT WAS MY FIRST DAY OF MED SCHOOL.
"THE DAY I STARTED THINKING OF MYSELF AS DOCTOR DONALD BLAKE.
"NINE-NINE. EASY TO REMEMBER. COINCIDENCE, REALLY, THAT TEN YEARS ON I FOUND MY STICK, BUT NINES AND COINCIDENCES SEEM TO HAPPEN A LOT AROUND ME..."
I'M SORRY, WHY DO YOU ONLY HAVE TEN YEARS OF MEMORIES?
WELL, IT GETS A LITTLE HAZY, BUT I GUESS THE SHORT VERSION IS...

"CALLOW YOUTH."

"WHICH I SUPPOSE NEATLY FRAMES THINGS IN A WAY MOST FOLKS CAN UNDERSTAND.
"I PARTIED PRETTY HARD WHEN I WAS A KID.
"I DRANK A LOT, GOT INTO A LOT OF FIGHTS...
"I GOT INTO SOME REAL TROUBLE, MAN.
"WHAT CAN YOU DO? EVERYBODY HAS STATIC WITH THEIR PARENTS AT SOME POINT, RIGHT?
"EVENTUALLY YOU JUST GROW UP..."
"AND OF COURSE YOUR PARENTS NEVER REALLY UNDERSTAND YOU SO YOU'RE JUST KIND OF ON YOUR OWN..."
THOR. OUR CHILD.
HOW WE HAVE MISSED YOU.
MOTHER. MOTHERS.
IT'S GOOD TO BE BACK.

IN AS MUCH THAT WE COULDN'T REMEMBER YOU.
WE VERY MUCH MISSED KNOWING THAT WE WERE MISSING YOU AS GREATLY AS WE WERE. ER...
MOTHERS. ALL IS WELL.
I COULD NOT REMEMBER YOU, EITHER. ANY OF YOU.
ANY OF THIS. MY OWN NAME, EVEN.
MY MIND IS MY OWN AGAIN, AT LAST, BUT I CONFESS IN MY ABSENCE SO MANY THINGS HAVE CHANGED AND...
...AND I DIED...
I WAS IN THE PLACE WHERE DEAD GODS GO. THERE WERE LEGIONS OF US THERE.
EVEN THOUGH I AM ONCE AGAIN ALIVE I FEEL LIKE A GHOST HAUNTING THE RUINS OF MY OLD LIFE...
YOUR OPULENCE!
HREIDMAR THE PARLIAMENTARY, REPRESENTATIVE OF ALL NIDAVELLIR, MA'AM--
--MADAMS--
--AH, SIR--
WE KNOW YOU, GOOD HREIDMAR, AND YOUR GOOD WORKS. WE REQUIRE YOU NOT TO STAND ON CEREMONY, FRIEND.
TELL US, DWARVEN SCHOLAR, WHY DO YOU PETITION YOUR ALL-MOTHER THIS DAY?
WELL, MA--
--ALL-MOTHER--
--I'VE A MYSTERY TO SOLVE THAT REQUIRES A CERTAIN...

"...IMPERIAL PRESENCE ON NIDAVELLIR..."
YOU SEE WHAT I MEAN?
I'M AFRAID I DON'T...
WELL, YOU SEE, I QUITE SIMPLY MUST BE ABLE TO CONTINUE CONSTRUCTION HERE, AND YET DEMOLITION REVEALED THIS CAVE.
NORMALLY WE'D SURVEY IT AND IMPLODE IT, REMOVE IT ALL, AND KEEP BUILDING BUT FOR THIS INSCRIPTION:
"LET THAT WHICH IS SEALED WITHIN THIS CAVE STAY SEALED HERE FOR ALL TIME AT THE BEHEST...
"...OF THE ALL-FATHER ODIN."
WELL, ODIN'S NOT AROUND ANYMORE. IS HE?
WHAT DO YOU WANT ME TO DO, HREIDMAR?
SURELY THERE WAS ONCE GOOD REASON TO SEAL IT BUT WE'VE NO IDEA WHAT THAT IS NOW. WE'D LIKE TO OPEN IT AND FIND OUT WHY.
SO, QUITE FRANKLY, I'D LOVE YOU TO BASH THE OBSTRUCTION IN AND CLEAR THE CAVE SO WE MIGHT FINISH OUR AQUEDUCT.
I CAN DO THAT.

CHEERS.
SO YOU DO HAVE MEMORY OF FAMILY, OF SOME KIND OF UPBRINGING.
YOU MADE IT SOUND AS IF YOU SIMPLY FOUND YOURSELF PART AND PARCEL A MEDICAL STUDENT...
IT'S CONFUSING. I WAS SPEAKING METAPHORICALLY. KIND OF.
MY MEMORIES BEFORE THAT NINTH DAY OF THE NINTH MONTH ARE ALL FAKE.
I WASN'T ALIVE BEFORE THE NINTH. EVERYTHING IN MY HEAD IS LIKE...
LIKE THE LONGEST DREAM EVER. BUT I CAME TO LEARN THERE WAS REALLY NO ME BEFORE THAT.
I WAS JUST A VESSEL FOR SOMEBODY ELSE. AND WHAT I THOUGHT WERE MY MEMORIES...

"...REALLY IT WAS JUST HIS COVER STORY. HE WAS OFF HAVING ADVENTURES AND I WAS...I GUESS I WAS HIS SHADOW..."
FREIDMAR I WANT YOU TO STAY BACK.
PROBABL FOR THE BEST, YE

FOR ASGARDIA!
WHAT ENCHANTMENT IS THIS?
GRRHH--
WELL.
HELLO THERE.

GREETINGS FROM ASGARDIA.
--AH.
IS THAT YOUR BEST?
OOPH--
DIE, BEAST!
AS FO
YOUR F
BROTHE

THEIR BEST WILL NOT SAVE *THEM*, *EITHER!*
--NO--
--DAMN!

--AHH.
WELL.
A WHOLE LEGION SLUMBERS HERE.
SOME WELCOMING COMMITTEE THIS GARDEN OF STONES MAKES...
...ONE GETS THE FEELING OF BEING UNWELCOME IN FACT...

HM.
WELL THEN?
I'VE NOT THE DAY TO WHILE AWAY.

ENCHANTMENTS BE DAMNED--
MJOLNIR! TO MY HAND--
GRRAAAH!
NO--
NO

VERY WELL.
NEXT?
NEXT?

STAY DOWN!
MORE SIMPLE TO SHATTER YOU DEMONS BEFORE THE LIGHT GRANTS YOU THE GIFT OF MOTION--
--THAN DEAL WITH YOU OTHERWISE--
FFWUH

COME ON, THEN--
COME ON!
GRRAAAHH--!

UM.
HELLO IN THERE? HELLO?
THOR...?
YOU WERE IN THE MIDDLE OF A SENTENCE AND RATHER ABRUPTLY STOPPED TALKING.
"FREIDMAR I WANT YOU TO--" YOU SAID, AND THEN TRAILED OFF.
A MYSTERY INSIDE OF A MYSTERY THEN, EH?
VERY WELL.
FREIDMAR THRIVES ON MYSTERY! ON--
OH NO.
OH MY GOODNESS NO.

BASSARDS... COMMME...
...COME ONNN YAA BASSARDS...
WE'VE FREED THE MARES.
"IN SHORT IT'S ALL A NIGHTMARE..."

...AND IT'S NOT EVEN MINE.
SO THAT, REALLY, IS WHY WE'RE HERE. THAT'S WHAT I WANT TO TALK ABOUT.
I'M AFRAID I DON'T ENTIRELY UNDERSTAND.
YOUR LIFE, YOUR MEMORIES.. THEY'RE NOT YOU OWN. WHAT DO YO THINK I CAN DO ABOUT IT?
YOU CAN DO EVERYTHING ABOUT IT. DON'T YOU GET IT?
I KNOW WHO YOU ARE, I'M SAYING. I REMEMBER EVERYTHING THAT HE REMEMBERS.
I KNOW WHO YOU ARE.
AND IF I CAN'T HAVE MY LIFE, THEN I WANT HIS.
MAKE ME A GOD AGAIN, ENCHANTRESS.
AND YOU CAN HAVE MY SOUL.

WELL NOW, DR. DONALD BLAKE.
FINALLY YOU'VE SAID SOMETHING THAT MAKES SENSE...

DEAR CYRUS HAIL SATAN!
EVERYTHING HERE SUCKS. NOW.
NO SURPRISE. I KNOW. ALL I WANT
TO DEDICATE MY LIFE + SOUL TO
MAKING DECONSECRATOR THE
BRUTAL BAND IN THE LAND AND
WE NEED TO TALK ABOUT JEFF, MRS. FISCHER, BECAUSE I'M WORRIED HE'S GOT HIMSELF OFF-TRACK EVER SINCE...
..WELL, SINCE CYRUS WAS SENT WAY. BUT HONESTLY HE WAS ON SLIPPERY SLOPE BEFORE THAT."
HE AND CYRUS PRETTY MUCH ONLY HAD EACH OTHER, NOW WITH CYRUS GONE...
...WELL, JEFF'S GRADES ARE IN FREE-FALL AND THE DISCIPLINE ISSUES ARE UP. HE'S BEEN GETTING INTO FIGHTS...
"...AND VANDALIZING EVERYTHING HE SEES, WRITING THAT BAND NAME OF HIS.
"AND MAYBE WE SHOULD HAVE TALKED ABOUT THAT SOONER, I DON'T KNOW. BUT...
"BUT THAT GIVES YOU SOME CONTEXT FOR WHERE HE'S BEEN AS A STUDENT HERE THE LAST FEW WEEKS.
So I got into it with Travis Ward and his Rampagin Rednecks today.
"AND IT BRINGS US TO TODAY'S INCIDENT..."

NOW, WE DON'T USE THE WORD "BULLYING" HERE AT NORTHERN BROXTON, WE CALL IT "UNRESOLVED CONFLICTION."
AND LATELY JEFF AND ANOTHER STUDENT, TRAVIS WARD, HAVE SEEMED TO HAVE A GOOD BIT OF UNRESOLVED CONFLICTION BETWEEN THEM BOTH...
"APPARENTLY THERE WAS ANOTHER CONFLICTION INCIDENT ACTION REPORT TODAY JUST AFTER LUNCH."
JEFF HAD BROUGHT THIS TASER ON TO CAMPUS TODAY.
DO YOU KNOW ANYTHING ABOUT THIS? WHERE HE MIGHT HAVE GOTTEN SUCH A THING?

ELSEWHERE...
TCH.
FASCINATING. IN FACT, I WONDER IF--
--!
AHH... HELLO?
IS SOMEONE THERE?
COME, COME NOW, I HEARD YOU.
YOUR PRESENCE HERE IS QUITE AGAINST THE RULES, I'M AFRAID. I AM THE ONLY ONE ALLOWED IN THE INFINITE LIBRARY, YOU SEE...
HELLO?

GGRRAAHH!
HAH.
YOU THERE. BOOKISH DWARF. I KNOW YOU.
YES. HREIDMAR, SIR. YES. I...I BELIEVE YOU MAY, YES...
...WHAT IS THIS PLACE?
A ROOM FULL OF THINGS THAT DARED ATTACK ME.
WHO CARES?
NO, NO, THERE'S SOMETHING WRONG HERE, SOMETHING IMPOSSIBLE...
...I THINK WE--
OH NO.
I CAME TO YOU. IN ASGARDIA. REMEMBER...?

"THERE WAS A CAVE. SEALED.
"BY THE DECREE OF ODIN. BUT WE...WE SMASHED IT OPEN AND WE..."
WE'RE DREAMING. WE SMASHED OPEN THE SEALED CAVE AND...
...AND WE FREED THE MARES. WE'RE ASLEEP AND TRAPPED WITHIN THE MARE'S NEST, DREAMING...
THOUGH IT DOES FEEL LIKE A DREAM. SHIFTING AND CHANGING AND... AND THESE THINGS WERE ANIMATING, TRYING TO KILL ME...
THE MARES WERE MYTHICAL, EVEN FOR A PEOPLE LIKE US WHO ARE SEEMINGLY MADE OF MYTHS.
...D WITHOUT ...ING A FINGER ...EY'VE FELLED US BOTH.
ALL RIGHT, SO? SO WE SLEEP. SO WE DREAM.
BUT IS IT MY DREAM OR YOURS?
WHO CARES? WE KEEP DREAMING UNTIL WE WAKE UP.
WHAT'S THE WORST THAT CAN HAPPEN?

NIDAVELLIR.

DGARD.
DR. BLAKE.
ARE YOU AWAKE?
MMPH.
GOOD.
GOOD MORNING, DOCTOR...
AMORA-- NCHANTRESS--
WHAT ON ARTH HAVE DONE TO BE REATED LIKE THIS...?
HMM.
NOTHING. YET...BUT LATER?
LATER I WILL CARVE A MAP OF PAIN ACROSS YOUR FLESH AS IT BOILS AND BURSTS.
WITH THE DEI-FORMING YOU ARE ABOUT TO ENDURE...THIS SEEMED THE LEAST I COULD DO.
HUNGRY?

HOW, AHH--
SHH.
OBSERVE.
AN APPLE. THE APPLE.
FOOD OF THE GODS, BLAKE. BETTER THAN ANYTHING YOU CAN CONCEIVE OF EATING.
GROWN BY GODS FOR GODS, BLAKE. YOU SHOULDN'T EVE SEEING IT, LET ALO TOUCHING--
AND THOR-- DOES THOR EAT THESE APPLES?
HE HAS, YES.
SURELY HE WILL AGAIN.
THEN SO SHALL I.
MMPH, ENCHHANNTR
YOU WERNFF KIDDIN--
HUH.
HURTS.
IT'S FOR GODS, BLAKE. AND YOU ARE NOT A GOD YET... BUT NOW YOU ARE ON YOUR WAY.
I'D PRAY FOR SOMEONE TO HELP YOU BUT NO ONE WOULD LISTEN...

AH... THOR?
I'VE JUST HAD A THOUGHT.
I'M URE YOU HAVE.
HAH. YES. WELL.
IF THIS IS A DREAM... THERE IS NO PRACTICAL GEOGRAPHY AROUND US.
MEANING-- WE'RE DREAMING THIS. THE DARK, THE CORRIDOR.
MOMENTS AGO, THAT YOU WERE IN A CORRIDOR.
WELL NOW IT HAS CHANGED. KEEP UP AND TREAD CAREFULLY.
I'M TRYING, I'M TRYING...
MY POINT IS THAT IF YOU THINK OF SOFT PILLOWS AND PELTS OF THE FINEST FURS PERHAPS WE'D BE IN BED RATHER THAN A DUNGEON.
MY POINT, THUNDER GOD, IS THAT YOU'RE WANDERING BLIND, EXPECTING HORRIBLE THINGS AND SO--
--HORRIBLE THINGS ARE WHAT WE FIND.
STOP. TALKING.
THERE. BEFORE US. LOOK.
THERE'S AN ANTECHAMBER AHEAD AND I HEAR...
...SCURRYING...

VILLAINS--!
THOR, NO--!
LOOK!--THE OTHERS OF NIDAVELLIR. OTHER BUILDERS LIKE MYSELF. THESE MEN--I KNOW THESE MEN.
THEY'RE ASLEEP NOW, TOO. AS WE ARE.
IT WOULD APPEAR SO.
"THEN IF THE MARES HAVE FOUND THEIR WAY INTO NIDAVELLIR...
"IF THEY'VE FELLED YO
FELLOWS AS EASILY
THEY DID YOU AND I

"...THEN THEY WILL HAVE FOUND YGGDRASIL THE WORLD TREE.
"THEN THEY WILL HAVE FOUND A WAY TO THE OTHER REALMS."
CERTAINLY.
WERE I A BETTOR I'D PUT MONEY ON OUR LITTLE NOCTURNAL ADVENTURE DOWN HERE FINDING ITS CAST EXPANDING WILDLY IN A MATTER OF HOURS...

SO THIS IS IT, MAN. I PACKED ONLY STUFF THAT FITS IN MY BACKPACK. EXTRA CLOTHES, DISCMAN, THE YNGWIE TABS AND MY GUITAR. AND THE GIBSON OF COURSE. BUT THAT'S ALL.
DECONSECRATOR
I ONLY TOOK 10 CDS. THE TEN GREATEST WORKS OF SUPREME METAL OF ALL TIME. NO ROOM FOR THE REST AND MUSIC IS ETERNAL AND ONE DAY WHEN I HAVE AN IPOD IT WILL ALL FIT THERE. THEY ARE:
1: ANTHR--WAIT I JUST HEARD MY DAD GET HOME.
MORE LATER.
OOPHA
HAIL SATAN.
HAIL SATAN.
HAIL SATAN.
"IT HURTS."

IT HURTS.
HELP ME.
SOMETHING LIKE THAT, PET.
SOMETHING LIKE THAT...
INSIDE ME.
FEELS LIKE THERE ARE BUGS INSIDE ME.
NO.
YOU WISHED TO TRANSFORM THE FLESH AND--
ASCEND!
WELL, DIVINITY COMES AT A PRICE.

GGUHHGKK
HEFF
HAH!
HEFF
I--
IT STOPPED? WHAT'S HAPPENING? WHAT'S GOING ON? WHAT AM I *LOOKING* AT...?

BEHOLD THE BIRTH OF A *GOD*...!
NNNOOOOOOOOOOO!

STAY CALM, PEOPLE. STAY ORDERLY.
KEEP IT TOGETHER, KEEP IT TOGETHER...
WELL?
WHAT DO YOU THINK?
I THINK THE CEILING MOVES.
PARDON?
I THINK THE CEILING MOVES. AWAY.
YES. SEE? WATCH THE LIGHT.
EVERYTHING IN DARKNESS SHIFTS. RECONFIGURES.
OH...OH, MY. THAT GOES AGAINST EVERYTHING RATIONAL AND REASONABLE.
WAIT-- THAT. THAT'S IT. WHAT YOU...
TELL ME WHAT YOU MEAN BY THAT.
ONLY THAT...
WE'RE BUILDERS. ARCHITECTS, ENGINEERS... STRUCTURE IS WHO WE ARE, THOR. DESIGN.
THE IDEA OF STRUCTURE FOREVER MOVING AND GROWING IS POSITIVELY...
OH NO.
THIS IS OUR NIGHTMARE, TOO.

AAAAAAAA!!!
THERE IS SURFACE.
THERE IS A GROUND.
THERE IS.

THIS IS NOT A FALL INTO THE INFINITE!
NOTHING LASTS FOREVER!
THERE WILL BE EARTH BENEATH OUR FEET.
STONE FOR OUR BOOTS TO STAND ON.
THERE IS GROUND. THERE IS UP AND THERE IS DOWN.
WE ARE BETWEEN.
AH.
HELLO?
REMARKABLE. A COLLECTIVE DREAM? STUNNING. I HAD THOUGHT THAT YOU WERE CONTROLLIN THE DREAM--YOUR WIL IS SO FEROCIOUS I COULD HARDLY CONCEIVE OTHERWISE AND YET--
YET HERE WE ALL ARE.
IMAGINE A RACE THAT COMMUNICATES NOT WITH WORDS OR SYMBOLS OR GESTURES...BUT WITH DREAMS.
IMAGINE IF THAT WAS YOUR LANGUAGE. COMMUNAL...SHARED... NARRATIVE EXISTING IN A CONJOINED DREAMSPACE.
HOW WOULD YOU WARN INVADERS IF YOU ONLY SPOKE THAT WAY?
I'D GIVE NIGHTMA

YES.
YOU WOULD.
NO NO NO NO--
KEEP IT OUT OF YOUR HEAD, THUNDER GOD!
ALL OF YOU! CLEAR YOUR MINDS!
WE ARE SAFE AS LONG AS WE THINK OF NOTHING!
IT'S LIKE I SAID BEFORE-- WHY NOT THINK OF PELTS AND PILLOWS?
TOO LATE--
DON'T, THOR--DO NOT ALLOW YOUR THOUGHTS--
--TOO LATE--
HE'S HERE!

WHERE IS MY SON?
MY FATHER. MY NIGHTMARE.

UH.
DON'T FREAK OUT, JEFF.
BROXTON, OK.
BE COOL AND DON'T FREAK OUT.
SOMETIMES TOWNS JUST GET SPONTANEOUSLY DESERTED...

LOOK, BLAKE!
LOOK AT WHAT YOU HAVE WROUGHT!
ELSEWHERE.
NO!
NO! ENCHANTRESS! MAKE IT STOP!
MAKE IT STOP!!!

WHAT DID YOU DO, THOR?
WHAT DID YOU DO?
MARELOCK.
MY.
BOYYY.
I HAD A BAD DREAM...

KEEP THEM SAFE...
WHAT DO YOU THINK YOU'RE--
FAMILY AFFAIR, HREIDMAR. DON'T WORRY ABOUT IT.
FATHER!
DIE AGAIN FOR ASGARD!--
--AAA!
MY.
BOYYYY.

GGFFFUUUAAAA--
--AAAAALLLL RIGHT.
"FATHER."
MY BOY.
UT
WHETHER CAST BY YOUR SHELTERING HAND OR CLENCHED FIST, I HAVE SPENT MY LIFE CLAWING MY WAY FROM OUT OF YOUR SHADOW.
I WILL NOT DIE IN YOUR DARKNESS.
BOY.

CLOSED
UM.
HELLO?
MR. COBB?
UH. LITTLE BILL? ARE YOU--OH--
...WHOA.

--UUHHH!
OH MAN.
OH MAN OH MAN.
AAAAAAHH!
SOMEBODY HELP ME!

OH MAN.
OH PLEASE. PLEASE PLEASE--
OH MAN OH PLEASE COME ON COME ON--
YAAAHHHH--!
FINE. GO AHEAD. STARE AT ME.
I'LL STARE RIGHT BACK, Y'BUNCHA CREEPY LITTLE BASTARDS.
ZZZRK
"WAKE UP!"

BLAKE! OPEN YOUR EYES!
AM I NOT A GRANTER OF DREAMS? DID I NOT MAKE YOUR WISH COME TRUE?
ADMIT IT, BLAKE. MORE OR LESS, THIS IS EXACTLY WHAT YOU ALWAYS WANTED.
I...I DON'T...
DON' FEEL GUH... GOOD... FUH...
SHH.
MMPH.
DREAMS REALLY DO COME TRUE, DOCTOR BLAKE...
BEHOLD:
THE TRUTH OF YOURS AND THE MAN OF MINE...

MISTRESS.
I AM YOURS.
MY KEEP.
THIS
IS
A

"...NIGHTMARE!"
WHAT...
IS THIS?
HO-LEE--
DIE FOR ASGARDIA!
BUH.
FATHER, YOU TRULY ARE MY WORS NIGHTMARE.

GRRAAHHH--!
BUH!
DON'T DIE
'T DIE DON'T
E DON'T--
RUN, BOY--
--RUN!

STAY DEAD ALREADY--
--FOR ONCE AND FOR ALL!
THOR!!!
I WILL BRING EVERY LAST ONE OF THESE PILLARS DOWN ON YOU, OLD MAN, AND--
--NO--
WHAT A RIP-OFF.

AAAAH--!
WHOA--
MUH! BUH!
PARENTS.

MIRACLE OF MIRACLES--
WILL SOMEONE PLEASE TELL ME--
--WHAT THE HELL IS GOING ON?
WEIRD CREATURES THAT COMMUNICATE BY DREAMS RUN AMOK. YOU'RE DREAMING. WE'RE ALL DREAMING.
THEY SIT UPON ONE'S CHES OR SWARM AROU THEIR TARGETS AND INSPIRE A COMMUNAL NIGHTMARE.
MEANWHILE
...THE DIRE MONKS OF GUNDERSHEIM HAVE A PLAN--AN ONEIROMANCE--A DREAM SPELL--
--WHERE THIS CIRCLE O COLLECTIVE VISIONARIE WILL SUMMON A DREAM HERO--
GOOD, GOOD. THINK HARD.
I SHALL BE OUT THERE, FIGHTING AND DYING.

POWERFUL THINGS DOES THIS ONE SEE.
EXCELLENT! GO, BOY, GO WITH THEM...
SUMMON US A HERO, BOY. SIT HERE WITH YOUR OTHER WORLDLINGS.
I--I'M DREAMING THIS, RIGHT?
SOME MIGHT SAY A DREAM IS LIVING YOU INSTEAD.
NO IDEA WHAT THAT MEANS.
SIT. DWELL.
I MEAN, I'M SORRY, BUT I DON'T--
SIT!
AND DWELL.
GAAAAHHHHHHH
FOCUS, LITTLE BLOSSOMS OF THE WORLD TREE. ON STRENGTH. ON MIGHT.
FOCUS ON A HERO TO SAVE ALL OUR LIVES.
SUMMON FORTH THAT WHICH WILL SAVE YOU.

BUH!
OOOOPH--

YES! YES!
I SEE HIM! I SEE--
THE SKY FALLS! ASGARD'S HERO AND THE NIGHTMARE BEAST ARE CRUSHED!
YES! YES!
NO...

OH NO. OH NO...
WHAT...
WHAT HAPPENED?
THEY COLLAPSED THE CEILING UPON THEMSELVES. THOR AND HIS... "FATHER"...
WHAT HAPPENED IN THERE? YOU WERE SUPPOSED TO DREAM US UP A HERO TO SAVE THOR AND THE REST OF OUR SORRY SOULS.
I DUNNO! I JUST--THEY SAID THINK ABOUT A HERO, SO I THOUGHT--
--OH GOD, I THOUGHT ABOUT HIM...
WHO? WHO?
OUR--OUR ALBUM.
I DREAMED ABOUT THE G ON THE COVER OUR FIRST ALB I COULDN'T HELP IT...
I SUMMO

HAIL SATAN!
...THE DECONSECRATOR...

IDGARD.
THAT...
THAT WAS SUITABLY EPIC.
AS WELL IT SHOULD HAVE BEEN.
WHAT... NOW?
THANK GOD YOU'RE FINALLY FINISHED.
GARDIA.
I WANT TO AKE YOU TO ASGARDIA...

I...
I THINK I MADE YOU, DUDE.
MARELOCK.
hail satan.
YEP.
YOU'RE JUST LIKE HOW WE *DREW YOU*...

DECONSECRATOR
"ME AND CYRUS ARGUED FOR WEEKS ABOUT WHAT WE SHOULD CALL OUR BAND BUT THE ONE THING WE AGREED ON...
"...WAS THE COVER FOR OUR FIRST ALBUM. AND WITH THAT CAME THE NAME..."
I GOTTA SAY THE ANVIL-ON-A-STICK, THING, MAN, IS AWESOME.
SO IF YOU CREATED THIS... CHARACTER... AND HE NOW HAS SOMEHOW INHABITED THOR...
HEN WHAT HALL WE DO?
OH, MAN, I WOULD START RUNNING.
HAIL SATAN!
RUN!!!

HAIL SATAN!
WHY WOULD ANYBODY THINK OF THAT?
BECAUSE IT'S AWESOME WHEN IT'S NOT TRYING TO KILL YOU--?
WHAT IS IT? WHAT DOES IT WANT?
DECONSECRATOR IS--LIKE--IT'S--
--IT'S METAL.
IT'S--LIKE--EVERYTHING METAL. THE BLACKEST OF DEATH METAL, MAN.
LIKE THIS--JUST--CONSUMING--RAGING--UNSTOPPABLE... DESTROYING...
JUST EVERYTHING--LIKE--STUPID PEOPLE AND LAME CRAP AND LIKE--LIKE--REDNECKS AND DRUNK DADS AND...
...DECONSECRATOR'S ALL ABOUT DESTROYING EVERYTHING. JUST, LIKE, FOREVER.
OH NO.

ASGARDIA:
E MARE VE BEEN FREED.
ASGARDIA-- TO MY SIIIIIIIIDE!
HMMPH.
THAT CAN'T BE GOOD.

THERE ARE SOFT SPOTS BETWEEN WORLDS. ONE NEEDN'T RELY SOLELY ON THE WORLD TREE TO MOVE FROM ONE TO THE NEXT.
THIS IS ONE OF THOSE PLACES. FROM HERE, THE DALES OF MIDGARD...
...TO THE DEPTHS OF HEL. FROM THERE FINDING ASGARDIA'S DOORWAY IS SIMPLE.
THERE'S A BRIDGE...
TURN ME AROUND. I CAN'T SEE WHAT SHE'S TALKING ABOUT.
WHAT?
WHAT IS SHE DOING? I CAN'T TELL.
THIS WAY.
HEL AWAITS.

SOMETHING'S AMISS.
I WOULDN'T KNOW.
SILENCE, NATTERING CUCKOLDED HEAD.
WHAT? WHAT? HOLD ME UP, DAMMIT, I CAN'T SEE WHAT'S...
HELA HAS FALLEN...

THIS IS WRONG.
THE MARE WERE SUPPOSED TO BE CONTAINED...
THEY HAVE NO LANGUAGE, YOU SEE, BUT FOR COMMUNICATION IN DREAM.
THE LAST TIME THEY ENCOUNTERED AESIR AND VANIR THEY HAD NEARLY LULLED ALL OF THE NINE WORLDS INTO SLUMBER.
THEY THOUGHT Y WERE BEING VADED. THEY ETALIATED E ONLY WAY HEY KNEW HOW.
THEY TRAPPED US ALL IN A COLLECTIVE NIGHTMARE.
ODIN SIMPLY SEALED THEM ALL INSIDE A CAVE NEVER TO BE OPENED AGAIN.
THIS WAS BEFORE SO MANY OTHER THINGS...VERY FEW OF US REMAIN OF THAT TIME...
TT. NIGHTMARES.
I WILL SHOW YOU NIGHTMARES...

no--
--how dare you--
--how dare--
hail satan

SWEET DREAMS. LOOK.
STOP! STOP! GET IT AWAY--
HAH.
IS DEAD. DON'T WORRY.
GGRRAAHH!!!
MY WORD.
THE MARE HAVE BEEN FREED, HELA. THOUGH NOT BY ANY OF MY DOING.
I SUSPECT THEY'VE RUN RIOT ONCE MORE...

WHAT...DO YOU WANT... AMORA?
A SHORT CUT. PASSAGE, IS ALL, FROM HERE TO ASGARDIA. I'VE A GIFT FOR THE GOD OF THUNDER.
AND I FELT IT UNWISE TO TREAD SO WITHOUT PERMISSION.
HOW WISE.
AND WHO IS YOUR COMPANION?
MY KEEP. THE KEEP.
AN OLD FRIEND OF THOR'S IN A NEW FORM.
OH! SO THIS KEEP IS...
HE'LL KILL YOU FOR THIS. OR WILL WANT TO.
WILL HE? YOU DETECT A VEIN OF EMPATHY WITHIN HIM THAT I DO NOT.
LET HIM TRY.
I'M RIGHT HERE.
TALKING ABOUT ME LIKE I'M NOT RIGHT HERE...
YOU MAY GO. YOU KNOW THE WAY AND I SUSPECT YOU'D TAKE IT EVEN IF I FORBADE.
GO FORTH TO ASGARD.
GO FORTH AND RAISE HEL.

HURRRH.
HAIL. HAIL SATAN. HAIL--
RATHER SINGULAR IN HIS FOCUS, IS HE NOT?
SHUT UP, DUDE! DECONSECRATOR'S AWESOME!
WHEN HE'S NOT TRYING TO KILL ME.
MORE AND MORE RACES FROM THE REALMS KEEP JOINING US.
THE MARE MUST HAVE FOUND THE WORLD TREE...
NO WONDER THEY WERE SEALED IN A TOMB.
AAAHHH!!!
HH.
HH.
HHHH--
THOR.
WE ARE NOT AMUSED.

HAAAIL
SILENCE--
WELL?
WHAT SAY YOU NOW?
MMMUH.
MOTHER.
THANK YOU.

CAREFUL, BOY.
AND GIVEN HALF A MOMENT--
--CHANGE.
THINGS ARE... ARE NOT WHAT THEY SEEM HERE. A NIGHTMARE DIPPED IN HONEY.
THINGS ADHERE HERE, GET TANGLED...

SO THAT WHERE ODIN PUT THE AREFOLK.
IT WOULD APPEAR.
...THERE WAS A PLAN. MONKS. ADEPTS. THIS BOY, HIS VISIONS--
INVARIABLY THE DREAM ASSERTS ITSELF AGAIN AND THINGS GO UPSIDE DOWN.

"ONE CANNOT FIGHT A DREAM, THOR, ANY MORE THAN ONE CAN WRESTLE A BLANKET INTO SUBMISSION.
"THE ONLY ESCAPE IS LUCIDITY. IS RETURNING TO THE WAKING WORLD."

THOR? ARE YOU...
I AM HOLDING MY HAMMER IN MY HAND.
"I CAN FEEL THE HANDLE AGAINST MY PALM. ITS WEIGHT.
"I CAN FEEL MY HAMMER IN MY HAND."
I CAN FEEL IT, I CAN--
--MOTHERS. MOVE BACK PLEASE.
"THE HAMMER IN MY HAND, THE HAMMER IN MY HAND, THE--"
--HAMMER IN MY HAND, I CAN FEEL IT AND--
"--AND I AM THE GOD OF THUNDER AND--"

IDAVELLIR.
aaaaa!!!

BEHOLD ASGARDIA.
OH.
OH MY.
WOWWWWWW.
WHAT HAPPENED HERE?

no--
--no no no--
While... tempting... believe me, I understand...
...this is not why we came here.
There. The royal spire. That is where we need to go.
Come, come, this way--
OH...HEY... IT'S SIF, YOU TWO. THIS IS REALLY BAD--
Stop right there.

THE ALL-MOTHER ARE IN NO STATE TO RECEIVE CALLERS.
SO TELL ME--
--HOW MAY THE FIRST SON OF ASGARD HELP YOU?

17

I WILL END YOU.
MANY HAVE TRIIIIEEUUUUPH--

BOYS.
BOYS.
BOYS.
IT TOOK E FOREVER T I FINALLY IGURED IT UT, THOR.
IF I COULDN'T FIND THE MAN REAT ENOUGH R ME I'D JUST AVE TO MAKE HIM.
I USED SNAKES AND SNAILS AND A TALE OF THE BOY BY WHOM THE GOD OF THUNDER FORGOT...
OF AT...
...WOMAN...
...DO YOU BABBLE?
THOR!
THOR. STOP FIGHTING.

I... KNOW THAT VOICE.
YEAH.
YEAH YOU DO.
BLAKE--?
AWW, LOOK AT THAT, HE REMEMBERS.
HAHAHA HAHAHA HA HA HAHAHA
HOW THIS

ARELOCK.
MADAMS ALL-MOTHER...
WE'VE JUST MADE A TERRIBLE MESS OF THINGS, I'M AFRAID.
GOOD HREIDMAR, ACCEPTING BLAME WHERE THERE IS NONE SOLVES THE PROBLEMS OF NO ONE.
'TIS A PROBLEM FOR ALL THE NINE REALMS, IT WOULD APPEAR.
WELL, ABOUT THAT. THE REALMS ARE HOME TO POWERFUL BEINGS AND THOSE BEINGS HAVE POWERFUL DREAMS.
AND STAGGERING NIGHTMARES.
THE SENSITIVES SNIFFED OUT BY OUR DIRE MONKS WERE MEANT TO--
--OH NO--
--NOT AGAIN!
NOT AGAIN, BOY! AWAKE!
"AWAKE WITH YOU!"
WHOA.

WHERE...
WHAT?
I WAS TRYING TO...
WHY HAVE YOU COME TO ASSAULT THE MAREFOLK, LITTLE DREAMER?
AND WHY SHOULD WE ALLOW YOU AND YOUR KIND TO LIVE?
OH... CRAP.

AST TIME THE
OY SUMMONED
H AN INFECTIOUS
A THAT YOUR SON
S TAKEN BY IT. THE
OY THOUGHT OF
T AS A HERO...
HE IS GIFTED WITH SUCH VISIONS THAT I FEAR WHAT HE MAY SUMMON AGAIN LEFT TO HIS OWN DEVICES.
BOY.
HUMAN BOY. CAN YOU HEAR ME?
NO--!
ALL-MOTHER! MY WORD--!!!
ONE THOUSAND APOLOGIES, ALL-MOTHER, I KNEW NOT THAT IT WAS YOU, I--
I WOULD NEVER DARE TOUCH--OR STRIKE--YOUR ROYAL--
UH-OH.

I DON'T UNDERSTAND HOW THIS CAN BE. I...I WAS DONALD BLAKE. HE WAS ME.
THAT'S NOT THE WHOLE AND SIMPLE TRUTH OF IT THOUGH, THOR-- THINK ABOUT IT.
I HAD A LIFETIME OF MEMORIES BEFORE FINDING THE STICK IN THE CAVE THAT TRANSFORMED INTO MJOLNIR--
--AND TRANSFORMED ME INTO YOU. SOMETHING ABOUT THAT LAST ADVENTURE OF YOURS, THOUGH... SOMETHING ABOUT YOUR "DEATH..."
IT FREED ME FROM THE PRISON OF YO AND YOU... DIDN'T EVE NOTICE.
BLAKE. I HAVE BEEN...THERE HAVE...
MY LIFE IS NOT SIMPLE BORING. AND W IT MAY PAIN Y TO HEAR IT, Y ARE NOT AT T CENTER OF I
BUT YOU WERE AT THE CENTER OF MINE!
I...
YES. OF COURSE.

my, what antastic ats we have this torrid tle DRAMA.
AND YOU COMPLAIN I NEVER TAKE YOU ANYWHERE.
THOR--
THOR, DON'T! IT'S WHAT SHE WANTS--
OHHH, MAN.
I KNOW THAT LOOK. I USED TO HAVE THAT LOOK...
an.
ntend smash r very e in--

UNHAND HER!
OOOOPH.

YOU. GOLEM.
YOU WHO WERE ONCE SKURGE THE EXECUTIONER.
GGFFFUUUHHHH--!
NNNNO!!!
YOU'RE JUST A PUPPET SHAPED LIKE A MAN. A TOY.
NOTHING TO A GOD. AND THIS GODDESS SHOULD BE ASHAMED FOR LETTING YOU TOUCH HER.
GUURRRH.
GRRR.
RRRRRIGHT.
TRY AGAIN.
AMORA, I HATE YOU.

DO YOU KNOW, MAN-LING OF MIDGARD, HOW LONG WE HAVE BEEN BANISHED HERE?
WHAT-LING?
WE CAME AND WENT AS WE PLEASED. WE WERE FREE.
AND THEN DARED CRO ODIN.
WE WERE LIKE YOU ONCE, MAN-LING. THE MARES WERE CITIZENS OF THE REALMS IN THE TIME-BEFORE-TIME.
HE INSISTED HIS DREAMS WERE A PLACE TO REMAIN UNTRAVELED BUT REFUSED TO UNDERSTAND--
--THIS IS OUR ONLY WAY TO COMMUNICATE...
SO TELL US...
...IF THAT WAS OUR TREATMENT ONCE UPON A TIME...
...WHY-EVER WOULD WE DARE LET ANY BEINGS FROM ANY OF THE REALMS COME CLOSE ENOUGH TO HARM US AGAIN?
TO US YOU ARE MONSTERS.

I GUESS-- UHH--
--LIKE-- BECAUSE DREAMS? MAYBE? BECAUSE DREAMS ARE KIND OF WHAT MAKE US GREAT?
I HATE MY LIFE, MAN. I HATE IT RIGHT NOW SO BAD YOU DON'T EVEN--
THIS MUCH, AT LEAST.
IT JUST SUCKS NOW.
AND I KNOW IT'S JUST NOW BECAUSE I CAN DREAM OF BETTER STUFF. OUT THERE. AWAY. LATER.
CYRUS? HE'S, LIKE--MY BEST FRIEND? HE TRIED TO KILL HIMSELF. HE COULDN'T--THEY SENT HIM AWAY. HE'S ON DRUGS NOW.
THE NO-FUN KIND, I MEAN.
EVERY NIGHT I DREAM OF A LIFE I DON'T HATE. AND THAT'S KEEPING ME ALIVE RIGHT NOW.
I THINK EVERYBODY DOES AND THAT'S HOW ANYBODY EVER DOES ANYTHING AWESOME.
I CAN PROVE IT TO YOU. YOU WANT TO SEE SOMETHING AWESOME?
YOU GUYS AREN'T IN MY DREAM RIGHT NOW. RIGHT?
I...I'M PRETTY MUCH YOUR WHOLE ENTIRE NIGHTMARE.

HAH.
GOT A BIG MOUTH, LITTLE MAN.
SHUT IT FOR YOU.
THIS REALLY IS A TERRIBLE WAY TO RECEIVE GIFT-BEARERS, THUNDER GOD...
THINK YOU AND THAT HAMMER OF YOURS HAVE DONE ENOUGH DAMAGE.
NOW BE A GOOD BOY AND THANK US FOR YOUR GIFT...
GIFT?
OH, COME ON--YOU
TO HIM--
--ENCHANTRESS--
BLAKE--
THOR.
KEEP HITTING HIM, MY LOVE.

WHY HAVE WE AWOKEN TO THIS...
...OUTBURST...
IN OUR HALL?
FREYJA. GAEA... IDUNN.
WE WERE SIMPLY COMING TO DELIVER A GIFT UNTO THOR AND TO TAKE THE OPPORTUNITY TO REMIND ALL OF YOU HIGH AND MIGHTY OF "ASGARDIA"...
...ABOUT THOSE LITTLE ONES SO EASILY FORGOTTEN BY GODS AND GODDESSES.
IS THAT ME? IS SHE TALKING ABOUT ME NOW?
YOU'RE A BRAT, AMORA. AND YOU ALWAYS WERE A BRAT.
YOU--AND YOUR LATEST PET--ARE NOT WELCOME HERE FOR GOOD REASON.
SO BE GONE.
I AM YOUR POISON!
AND I SHALL SEEP INTO EVERYTHING YOU ARE.
THOR. REMOVE THIS TRASH.

AS YOU WISH, MOTHER.
HERE-- YOU'LL LIKE THIS TRICK.
I LEARNED IT FROM FATHER--!
AMORA!
HEAVENS.
OUT WITH YOU BOTH.

OOOOPH.
WHAT DID I DRINK?
THE WHOLE OF IT I SHOULD THINK, IF YOU FEEL LIKE I FEEL.
NOW--
--FOR BOTH OF YOU--
--GET OUT.
"WELCOME HOME.

"YOU RETURN FROM NIDAVELLIR AND THE MARELOCK WITH GOOD WORD, WE TRUST."
I DO AT THAT...
THEY WANT A VOICE IN THE PARLIAMENT OF REALMS, THEY WANT A PRESENCE. THEY WANT TO NOT BE ODIN-BOUND IN A CAVE ANYMORE...
THERE WILL BE PEACE. TO ENSURE IT, THEY GRANTED ME A BOON. NOW I'M IN THEIR DEBT.
UNLIKE THE THUNDER GOD TO HAVE A DEBT HANGING OVER HIS HEAD.
TELL US, THOR--WHAT COULD YOU POSSIBLY OWE THE MARES TO ENSURE PEACE BETWEEN OUR KINDS?
I...

D SO THE MARES
D FOR ME WHAT
HEY ALWAYS DO.
"THEY CRAFTED
A DREAM."

BROXTON, OK.
OKAY.
HERE GOES--
WHERE THE HELL HAVE YOU BEEN?
WELL?
ANSWER ME, YOU LITTLE--
--LITTLE--
I'M REALLY TIRED. I'M GOING TO BED.
YOU DON'T GET TO HIT ME OR MOM ANYMORE.
DEAR CYRUS,

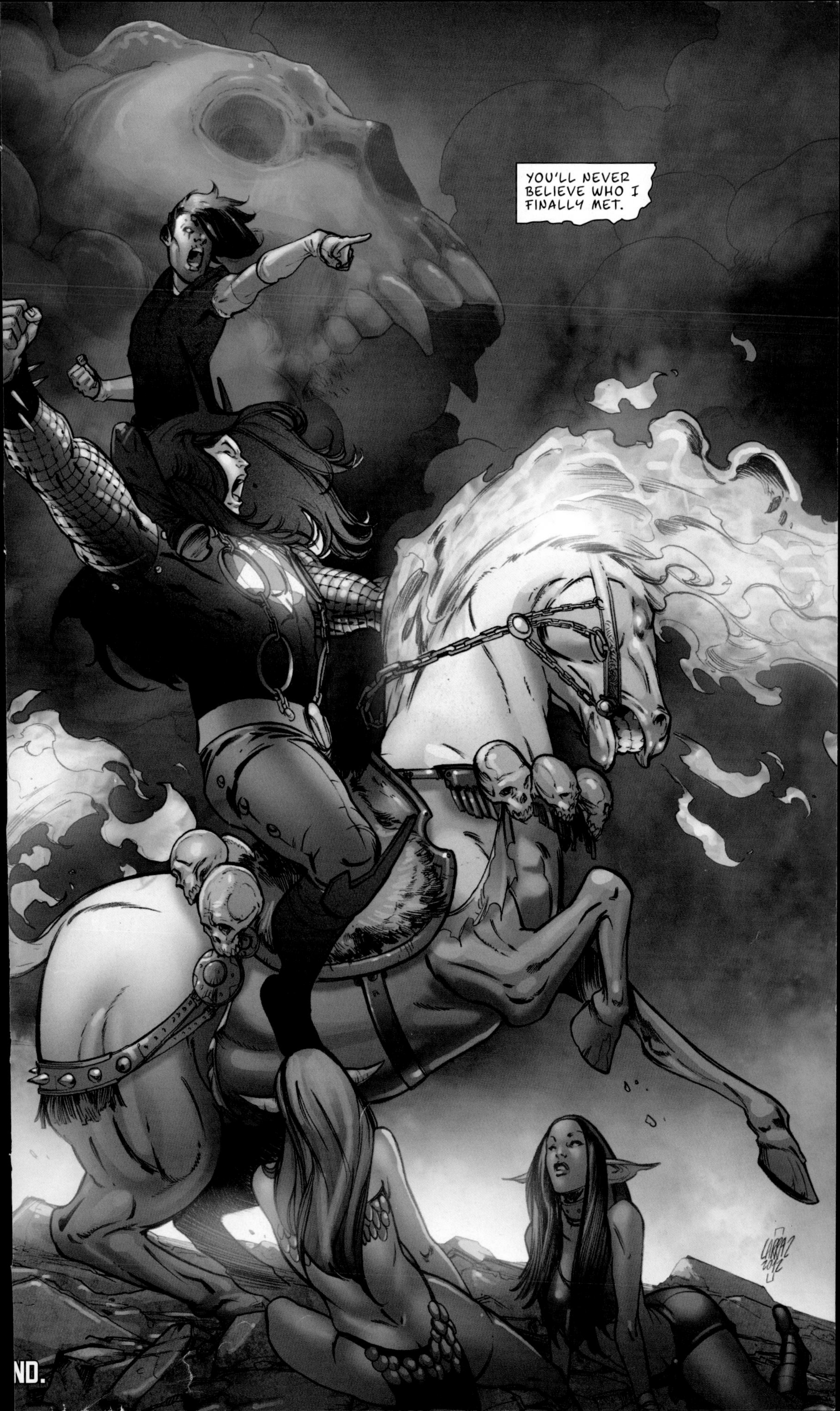
YOU'LL NEVER BELIEVE WHO I FINALLY MET.
ND.

#13 AVENGERS ART APPRECIATION VARIANT
BY RICHARD ISANOVE

#13 COVER INKS

#14 COVER INKS

#16 COVER INKS

"IT'S A BEAUTIFUL BOOK TO LOOK AT AND READ." *- A COMIC BOOK BLO*

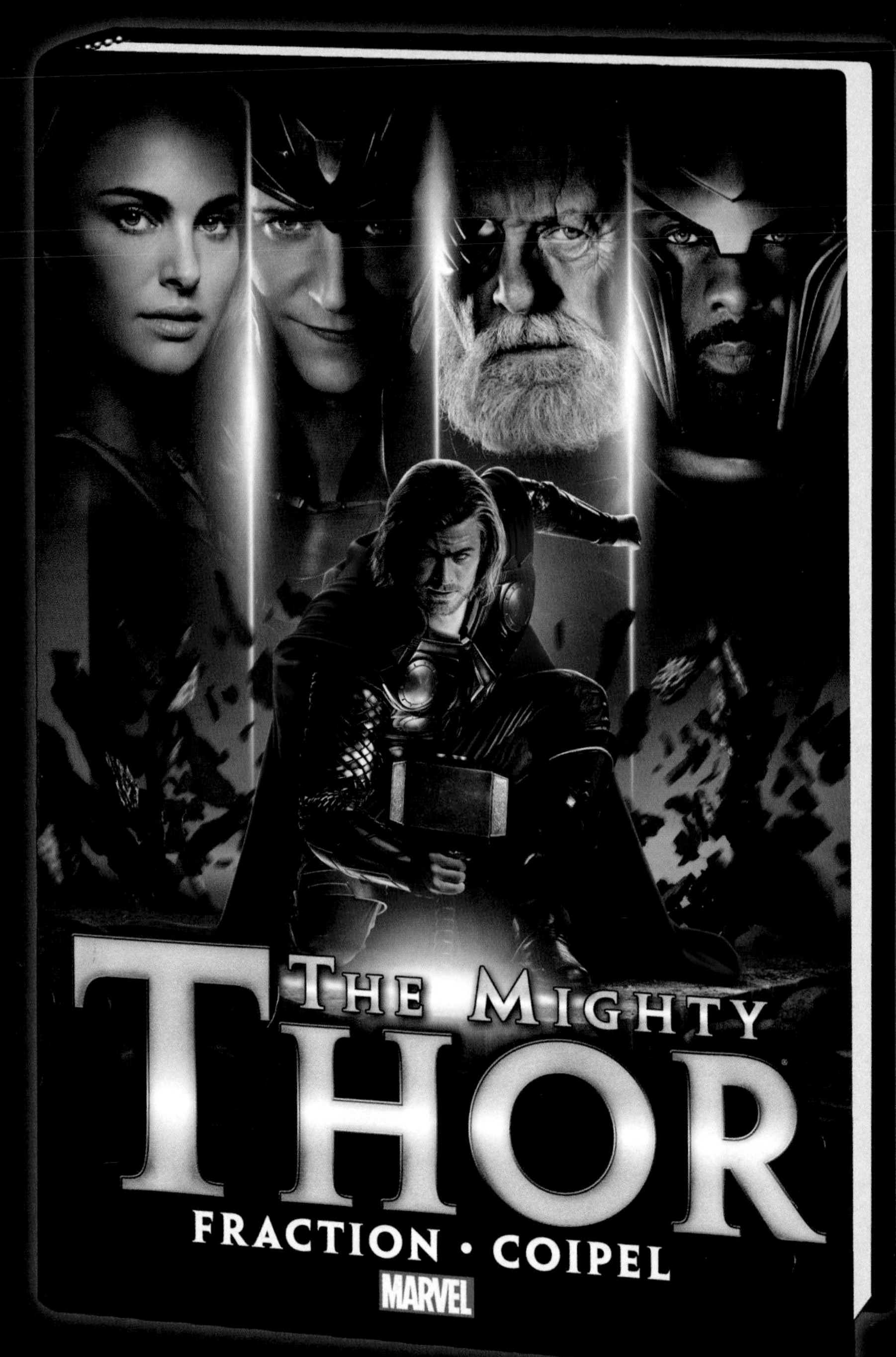

THE MIGHTY THOR BY MATT FRACTION VOL. 1 PREMIERE HC
978-0-7851-5691-8

ALSO AVAILABLE

THOR BY J. MICHAEL STRACZYNSKI VOL. 1 TPB
978-0-7851-1722-3

THOR BY J. MICHAEL STRACZYNSKI VOL. 2 TPB
978-0-7851-1760-5

THOR BY J. MICHAEL STRACZYNSKI VOL. 3 TPB
978-0-7851-2950-9

THOR BY KIERON GILLEN ULTIMATE COLLECTION TP
978-0-7851-5922-3

THOR: THE WORLD EATERS TPB
978-0-7851-4839-5

TM & © 2012 MARVEL & SUBS